SUPERIOR ANIMAL SENSES

HOW
DOLPHINS
AND OTHER ANIMALS
USE SONAR

Therese Shea

PowerKiDS
press.

Published in 2016 by The Rosen Publishing Group, Inc.
29 East 21st Street, New York, NY 10010

First Edition

Editor: Katie Kawa
Book Design: Reann Nye

Photo Credits: Cover Perrine Doug/Perspectives/Getty Images; p. 5 Lemonpink Images/Shutterstock.com; p. 7 (fish finder) Sebastien-Coell/iStock/Thinkstock.com; p. 7 (fisherman) Stephen Mcsweeny/Shutterstock.com; p. 9 Ricardo Canino/Shutterstock.com; p. 11 (dolphin) Tory Kallman/Shutterstock.com; p. 11 (orca) Tom Middleton/Shutterstock.com; p. 11 (narwhal) Paul Nicklen/National Geographic/Getty Images; pp. 13 (both), 22 (bat) Ivan Kuzmin/Shutterstock.com;p. 15 John Brown/Oxford Scientific/Getty Images; p. 16 feathercollector/Shutterstock.com; p. 17 John J Bangma/Science Source/Getty Images; p. 19 Erni/Shutterstock.com; p. 21 (radar) Eugene Sergeev/Shutterstock.com; p. 21 (whale) TAGSTOCK1/Shutterstock.com; p. 22 (whale) Shane Gross/Shutterstock.com.

Library of Congress Cataloging-in-Publication Data

Shea, Therese.
How dolphins and other animals use sonar / by Therese Shea.
p. cm. — (Superior animal senses)
Includes index.
ISBN 978-1-4994-0988-8 (pbk.)
ISBN 978-1-4994-1028-0 (6 pack)
ISBN 978-1-4994-1054-9 (library binding)
1. Sonar — Juvenile literature. 2. Echolocation (Physiology) — Juvenile literature. 3. Dolphins — Juvenile literature. I. Shea, Therese. II. Title.
QL737.C432 S54 2016
599.53 —d23

Manufactured in the United States of America

CPSIA Compliance Information: Batch #WS15PK: For Further Information contact Rosen Publishing, New York, New York at 1-800-237-9932

CONTENTS

Clever Dolphins

People love dolphins so much that they go to aquariums and on special boat rides just to see them. Dolphins charm us by doing tricks and leaping over waves. These **mammals** are known for their friendliness toward people as well as their cleverness.

Dolphins are also known for the noises they make. Scientists think dolphins make noises by moving air through body parts below their blowhole. They squawk, whistle, click, and squeak. However, this isn't just noise—it's how they talk! Dolphins make noises for other reasons, too. They use sound waves to **navigate**, find food, and avoid predators.

THAT MAKES SENSE!

Like people, dolphins may move certain body parts when they "speak."

Bottlenose dolphins, like the ones pictured here, seem to smile because of the shape of their mouth.

ECHO-WHAT?

"Sonar" is short for "sound navigation and ranging." Sonar is the use of sounds to find underwater objects and locations. People use sonar machines. They send out sounds, which travel as waves and bounce back once the waves hit something. This is called active sonar. Some kinds of sonar pick up sound waves coming from another source. This is called passive sonar. Scientists, the military, and fishermen all use sonar.

A dolphin doesn't need a sonar machine. It's in its body! Not only can dolphins use sounds to locate something in deep, dark water, they can tell its size, shape, speed, and **distance**. An animal's use of sonar is often called echolocation.

THAT MAKES SENSE!

An animal's sonar is also called biosonar. "Bio" means "life" or "living."

This fisherman is using a sonar machine to find fish in the water. A sound wave travels almost 1 mile (1.6 km) per second through water, which is faster than it travels through air.

UNDERWATER ECHOES

Dolphins are great at using echolocation. The dolphin makes a clicking noise. The sound goes out through the dolphin's forehead as a sound wave. This sound wave travels until it hits something. It then **echoes** back to the dolphin. The sound wave is **detected** by the bones in the dolphin's jaw and then its ears. The **information** sent through the echo goes to the dolphin's brain, which tells the dolphin about the object.

By using echolocation, the dolphin can tell what an object is, how fast it's going, and in what direction. A dolphin's echolocation is so good that scientists study it to find out how to improve man-made sonar.

THAT MAKES SENSE!

A dolphin's forehead is also called a melon.

A dolphin's biosonar usually works best to find objects less than 650 feet (198 m) away.

TOOTHED WHALES

Dolphins aren't the only animals that use echolocation. They're not even the only animals in the ocean that do! It's thought that most toothed whales use echolocation. What are toothed whales? They include dolphins as well as porpoises, orcas, pilot whales, sperm whales, narwhals, and beluga whales.

Not all toothed whales have the same echolocation abilities. For example, porpoises are **prey** for orcas. Porpoises' echolocation clicks may have become higher in frequency over many, many years until orcas couldn't hear them. However, an orca can still use its own echolocation to catch a porpoise snack!

THAT MAKES SENSE!

A sound wave's frequency is the number of times the wave is repeated over a certain period.

bottlenose dolphin

orca

Scientists think toothed whales are so good at echolocation that they may use it in place of sight. It's hard to see in the dark waters of the deep ocean!

narwhal

Bat Biosonar

Animals that live out of the water use echolocation, too. Much like dolphins and other toothed whales need echolocation in dark waters, most bats need echolocation because they're nocturnal. That means they're mostly active at night. They need to use echolocation to find food in the dark.

Bats make noises much like we do. They move air past **vocal cords**. The sound either comes out through their mouth or nose, depending on the kind of bat. The noise is such a high pitch that people can't hear it. Still, the sound travels as waves, bounces off an object, and echoes back to the bat.

THAT MAKES SENSE!

A sound's pitch is how high or low it is. Human ears can only hear sounds at certain pitches.

Many bats hunt and eat bugs. They use echolocation to find these bugs.

ECHO TO EAR

The echoing sound can tell a bat a lot about an object. Scientists think the folds in a bat's ears help it detect if the object is above or below it. A small object reflects, or sends back, less of the sound wave. A big object reflects a bigger sound wave and makes a stronger echo.

The pitch of the echo tells the bat what direction the object is moving. An object moving away sends back an echo with a lower pitch than the sound the bat made. An object moving toward the bat gives off an echo with a higher pitch.

THAT MAKES SENSE!

Bats make longer sounds and more kinds of sounds than dolphins when using echolocation.

A bat's eyes and ears work together to help it locate things in the darkness.

15

Oilbirds and Swiftlets

Some kinds of birds use echolocation, too. The most famous are the South American oilbirds, or guácharos. This bird lives in caves, leaving only to find food at night. Since the oilbird lives most of its life in darkness or very low light, echolocation helps it find its way around. It uses biosonar to navigate inside its cave and to find fruit outside the cave.

People can hear the echolocating sounds oilbirds make, unlike the biosonar sounds of dolphins and bats. An oilbird can make nearly 250 clicking sounds per second!

THAT MAKES SENSE!

Asian swiftlets are birds known for using echolocation, too. Like oilbirds, swiftlets live in caves and use echolocation to navigate in the darkness.

Asian swiftlet

Oilbirds are reddish brown and about 12 inches (30 cm) long. They have large, dark eyes.

Shrew Sounds

Scientists are still discovering animals that use echolocation. Shrews are one of these recent discoveries. These small, mole-like mammals have tiny eyes and poor eyesight, but they have excellent senses of smell and hearing.

Like many animals that use echolocation, shrews are mainly nocturnal. They make high-pitched sounds. Studies have shown that these sounds are used in echolocation to find out about surroundings and the best way to travel through them. Shrews may also use echolocation to find bugs and other small animals to eat. Shrews need to eat a lot to stay alive, so echolocation is very important for them.

THAT MAKES SENSE!

There are about 350 kinds of shrews. Most are about 2.5 inches (6 cm) long with a short tail.

Shrews are found across North America, some parts of South America, Africa, Europe, Asia, and Australia.

DISRUPTING THE SOUND

Unfortunately, echolocation doesn't help animals "see" everything. For example, echolocation doesn't detect some fishing nets, so dolphins and other small toothed whales can still be caught and killed. Also, boat motors and underwater drills make sounds that **disrupt** echolocation.

While we're not sure if people's actions affect bat echolocation, we do know that **wind turbines** kill nearly 900,000 bats per year. Bats, oilbirds, and shrews are also at risk when people take over their **habitats**. However, people can do things to help animals with biosonar. Turn the page to find out more!

THAT MAKES SENSE!

Bats may use sounds to "jam" other bats' echolocation to keep them from finding all the bugs in an area. Moths can make clicks to mix up bats hunting them, too!

Sonar used by navies has been tied to whales becoming trapped on beaches because it confuses the whales.

When building, people can make sure bats, oilbirds, and shrews have enough space to live.

Navies can change their use of sonar so it won't affect whale actions.

People can use less noisy boat motors in waters where echolocating whales live.

HELPING ANIMALS THAT USE ECHOLOCATION

Echolocation detectors near turbines can help control the turbines' speed and use, saving bats' lives.

Scientists can work on quieter methods of finding and removing oil underwater, so it doesn't disrupt dolphin and whale echolocation.

Fishermen can use nets with tools that dolphin and whale biosonar can "see" and avoid.

GLOSSARY

detect: To notice or discover something exists.

disrupt: To cause something to be unable to continue in the normal way.

distance: The space between two points.

echo: To make a repeating sound because of sound waves bouncing off an object. Also, the sound it makes.

habitat: The natural home for plants, animals, and other living things.

information: Knowledge or facts about something.

mammal: Any warm-blooded animal whose babies drink milk and whose body is covered with hair or fur.

navigate: To plan and follow a path from one place to another.

prey: An animal hunted by other animals for food.

vocal cords: Thin pieces of folded tissue in the throat that help make sounds.

wind turbine: A motor powered by the movement of air.

INDEX

WEBSITES

Due to the changing nature of Internet links, PowerKids Press has developed an online list of websites related to the subject of this book. This site is updated regularly. Please use this link to access the list: www.powerkidslinks.com/sas/dol